Surprised

by joy

A History of the Community
of the Servants of the Cross

1882-2004

by

Sister Jane of the Cross

British Library Cataloguing in Publication Data

**A catalogue record for this book is available
from the British Library**

ISBN 0-9534611-3-0

First published 2004, by
SMH BOOKS
Pear Tree Cottage, Watersfield, Pulborough,
West Sussex, RH20 1NG
Tel. 01798 831260

Typeset by Michael Walsh
MusicPrint, Chichester

Printed and bound in Great Britain by
RPM print & design, Chichester

DEDICATION

This Book is dedicated to
The Servants of the Cross, past and present,
our Associates, past and present,
and to all our Benefactors and Friends

The Sisters' Crosses

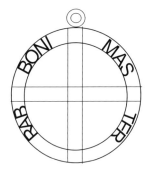

The Noviatiate Cross

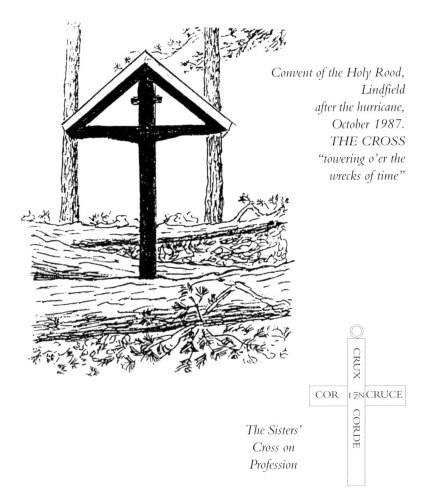

Convent of the Holy Rood,
Lindfield
after the hurricane,
October 1987.
THE CROSS
"towering o'er the
wrecks of time"

The Sisters'
Cross on
Profession

CONTENTS

PREFACE

Sometimes, the happiest things occur by complete chance – a serendipitous event. So it was, with my introduction to the Servants of the Community of the Cross.

Many years ago, a friend who was staying with me talked of when she had worked, as a teenager, at St Peter's Convent, in Woking. She said she would love to return, to see Mother Margaret Paul and the Sisters. She then rang the Convent, and we were invited to stay.

We were greeted, on arrival, by a Sister who led the way to a cottage called 'Redwood', where we were accommodated in great comfort, and made to feel very welcome.

During our stay, Reverend Mother asked about my occupation. When I told her it was book-keeping, she asked if I had any spare time. Sister Theodora, who had taken care of the work at Holy Rood Convent, Lindfield, had recently died and Mother Doris was desperately looking for a replacement. I told her Saturdays were my only free days.

Little did I know how much that visit would change my life, and the events I would be involved in. I was to meet lovely people, and kindness. Lasting friendships would be forged with the Sisters, Associates and Friends of the Community…

I met Mother Doris the Monday evening after our return (next day!). Driving from Uckfield to Lindfield, I felt apprehensive, but excited. Mother Doris took me into her office, which, I remember, had a most impressive carved wooden fireplace. She made me welcome, and spoke in a soft, gentle, clear voice, telling me all about the Convent. I had no hesitation in saying "yes" to being their Bursar, and have never regretted it. When I left, I was already looking forward to starting work on the Saturday – and seeing the Convent grounds in daylight.

My days at Holy Rood Convent were a great inspiration: getting to know the Sisters and working with them in many ways. They used to sit outside my office door, on a church pew, waiting their turn to come in for a chat. As they went away, I could hear the tip-tapping of their shoes on the beautiful, polished floors.

When I arrived, there was always a posy of flowers, mostly picked from their garden, on the beautiful Wellington chest in the office. Tea and coffee were brought in on a tray, on a hand-embroidered cloth, and soup arrived for lunch. I was truly spoilt!

One day, I was invited to lunch in the Guests' Dining Room, with the Chaplain, Father Hollowood. I discovered he had been Vicar of St Mark's Church, Hadlow Down, which my family attended when living in the parish, until I was seventeen. We also went to the school there. Father Hollowood had known my mother's brother, Charles Smith who was, and still is (after fifty-eight years!) the organist at St Mark's...

On Saturdays, after lunch, I would hear the Sisters' melodious voices in the distance, at choir practice, in preparation for Sunday Mass. I looked forward to that, and used to strain to hear them more clearly.

At the end of my working week, then spending Saturday at the Convent, far from feeling tired and depleted, I would go home feeling relaxed, and at peace.

In 1996, due to decreasing numbers of Sisters, and their increasing frailties, arrangements were made for the Sisters to move, and for the Convent to be sold. Mother Angela asked the Warden if I could attend the many meetings held during this period. At the very first, I was asked if I would become secretary to the Trustees. No time wasted there!

During winter, 2002-3, residents and staff at Marriott House contracted an infectious bug, and residents stayed in their own quarters for ten days, to try to stamp out the infection as quickly as possible.

With her ever-active mind, Sister Jane put this time to good use by compiling this History. What a splendid idea that was – and here is the fruit of her labours!

On a personal note:

Sister Jane,

I greatly admire your Spirituality and your wonderful work in putting together this book, with help from the memories of Mother Angela and Sister Margaret. I think the Book was one of God's plans for you, and I believe that those who read it will find it both interesting and a source of inspiration and comfort.

Wendy.

March 2004

Wendy Compton
Bursar and Secretary to the Trustees

Thou "Crux" to Servants of the Cross
    No ornate symbol art,
But very form and fashion of
    The Spirit of the Heart.

Thou hidden aim, and richest prize!
    Thou most familiar prayer!
With Thee plunged deep within my Heart,
    Heaven's anchorhold is there!

So Crux in Corde, Cor in Cruce,
    High up on the Cross
My Heart, transfixed by many a pain
    Finds joy in every loss.

O Thou the source and centre art
    Of all I hold most dear,
For always when the Cross is felt
    Then CHRIST Himself is near.

1

Names of the Sisters of the Servants of the Cross

Sisters		
	Harriet Mary	1882
	May	1882
	Georgina	1884
	Anne	1885
	Grace	1887
	Edith	1889
	Priscilla	1889
	Ellen	1889
	Marta	1892
	Gertrude	1893
	Eleanor	1895
	Elizabeth	1895
	Winifred	1903

The following sisters were still living when Sister Jane came into the Community, in 1959:

Sisters		
	Rosina	Bertha
	Pauline	Rhoda
	Jessica	May
	Stella	Hannah
	Mary Faith	Dorothea
	Louise	Lucy
	Lena	Mary Grace
	Olive	Christine Mary
	Mildred	Angela
	Helena	Edith Magdalene
	Janet Mary	Gertrude Anna
	Freda	Ethel
	Margaret	Jane
	Doris	Ruth
	Monica	Dorothy May

Part of Worthing Convent

The garden at Holy Rood, Worthing

Surprised by Joy

Bath chairs at the ready for an outing! Worthing

Findon High Street as it was – and still is

2

A History of the Community

We owe our Foundation to the work of Dean Walter Butler, of Wantage, and Mother Lucy, of the Community of St Mary the Virgin, Wantage, and our thanks go to all the Mothers and superiors supplied by them quite late in our life, in 1968, when Sister Dorothea became the first of our own Mothers.

The Society of the Servants of the Cross was founded in 1877. The Sisters of St Mary the Virgin were looking after girls at risk in Fulham. Soon, some of these girls wished to dedicate their lives, in a life of Reparation and Service. Dean Butler and Mother Lucy found a House there, where they could learn about the Religious Life.

On 20 February, 1882, Miss Harriet Jane Workman presented herself for Profession as Sister Harriet Mary of the Community of the Servants of the Cross. That was when our Community was founded. Ever since, we have kept 20 February as our Birthday Festival.

We were founded 'in order to give working-class girls an opportunity to consecrate themselves to Christ, in a Spirit of Reparation for their own sins, and those of the whole world'.

The Community's active work was caring for the sick and infirm.

In 1895, the Community moved to Worthing, in West Sussex, where their numbers increased. For a short time, they also ran a convalescent home for children, and I have heard stories of how they would all go down to the seaside, the children being pushed in bath chairs and wheelchairs, and have a lovely day out!

Around that time, the Community was asked by Bishop Michael Furze, Bishop of Johannesburg, South Africa, to help at the Jane Furze Hospital in Johannesburg (named after his daughter, who died there, as a child). It was hoped to run a Mission Hospital there. Three Sisters worked there for a year or so. They then had to return, owing to a shortage of Sisters at the Worthing Home.

For the same reason, a few years later, the work among invalid children had to be stopped. We were never a large Community in all our long years.

Worthing itself began to expand, and new buildings rose up, all round our Convent. When a noisy nightclub opened next door, we decided to move elsewhere!

Surprised by Joy

A plot of land was purchased in Findon, below the South Downs, not too far away but in wonderful surroundings. There, a large Convent and Home were erected, to accommodate sixty or more female patients – mostly terminal cases. The Convent for the Sisters was on one side and the Home, on the other, with a lovely, large Chapel in the centre.

The buildings were called Holy Rood Convent and Home, as were all our Convents, and the entrance was most imposing. In the extensive grounds, we had our own laundry and several houses, including the Chaplain's House.

As some of the Associates and Friends will remember, the gardens were beautifully laid-out with flower beds, and a Garth. This was a semi-circular open space, surrounded by a high privet hedge on three sides. Here, we could be secluded and private, and it was a favourite spot in our Day Retreats.

There was some orchard ground, where fowl were looked after, and beehives were tended. At the back of the laundry building was a big vegetable garden, which provided us with fresh vegetables and fruit.

It was a delightful place, where we lived for thirty-odd years, serving our patients and fulfilling our Vocation. (More is written about that, further on in this Booklet.)

Between 1956 and 1966, several Sisters died, and with others ageing and no young Novices coming in, we found we could not carry on. What was to be done?

In 1960, we had purchased a smaller House at Lindfield, near Haywards Heath, still in West Sussex, which the East Grinstead Sisters wished to sell. In a wonderful way, we had unexpectedly received a large sum of money – the exact sum required to purchase this place. We carried on looking after the retired ladies who had been left there by the other Sisters. St Margaret's House became our Branch House. Two or three Sisters ran the place, and lived their dedicated lives of service and worship there.

When we found we could not continue living at Findon, we contacted builders to add on further rooms at Lindfield, to accommodate the whole Community. They matched up the old and the new in a most attractive way.

On a certain day in 1967, we made the move to Lindfield, after placing all our dependants in other nursing homes in the area. The work on some of the rooms had not been quite completed when we left Findon, so some of our Sisters had to be 'housed out' for a time. Several of us were sent to Wantage, to serve in the Infirmary. Others went to families and friends who could have them. At first, our furniture had to stay under tarpaulin coverings on the lawn at Lindfield, until we could find a place indoors for it all!

We reached our sleeping quarters over planks until our cells were completed and everything was secure, and we could all be together again.

The arrangement of the original kitchen and pantry was altered, so for a time we had our meals in what had been the Guests' Dining Room. This reverted back as time went on, and we had a new kitchen and Refectory on the far side of our building.

Meanwhile, the Roman Catholic Sisters of Zion were settling down in Findon. They had visualised it as a Home for all the elderly Sisters from their many Convents. The Stalls in the Chapel were removed and it was filled with chairs, as in a Church. We were invited over there on one occasion and found it all much changed. The Chapel looked different, but was very bright and beautiful. Unfortunately, things did not work out for the Sisters of Zion. Some years later, we heard that the convent had been sold, and our lovely building, pulled down to make room for a lot of houses and, I think, a school. I learned that they had put up a plaque where the Convent had been, so that it would be remembered in years to come.

On a visit to a friend in the summer of 2000, we could hardly recognise the village and the lane leading up to the Convent during our days there. But the village square was still there, and the road up to the Cemetery, along which we used to walk behind the biers to bury our Sisters in their enclosed Garth in the Cemetery. Once, I recall, we did this in thick snow! … (More is written about this, further on in the Booklet.)

When we left Findon, we had taken our Calvary to Lindfield. It was a lovely, life-size Statue of our Lord, made of black metal material, on a wooden Cross, set on a white cement and brick base, with steps leading up. We placed it on the front lawn of the Convent.

At first, we used the former large Guest Sitting-Room as our Chapel, until our Chapel could be built. Later, the sitting-room was divided, to provide a Work Room and a Craft Room-cum-Reception Room.

We had four permanent guests to care for, until they needed professional daily and nightly nursing care. We also had short-term guests for holidays or periods of convalescence.

We offered ourselves to provide nursing assistance in the area, to help pay our way. Much of the housework we did ourselves, along with two paid cooks to cover the day, and one or two helpers for House work. This was our way of helping neighbours, by providing jobs to earn a little money.

Soon, one or two of us were doing night nursing in the homes in the village, so that daughters could get a good night's sleep now and then, or a little holiday away, knowing their loved ones were being cared for in the night, as well as by others in the daytime.

We helped, too, in local nursing homes for a few hours, and one Sister sometimes did night duty at a home for mentally handicapped children. We were called upon to help at the Holy Cross Convent, too, for night duty for sick Sisters there.

All this filled a gap until, with the help of the Diocese, and some financial help from the Fathers of Cowley: our Wardens for some years while they could spare someone to be so, we were able to build St. Richard's Hall, and to furnish it appropriately. The Hall became a well-known Retreat and Conference Centre for the Diocese of Chichester.

When we met up with former Priests and Friends, they would recall particularly their Post-Ordination Retreats and, afterwards, their Post-Ordination Training Days – POTS, we called them! They also spoke of wonderful meals they were given on those days, from our kitchen – especially the rice pudding! Some even took a bowl home with them.

We also hired out the Hall for various functions, old age group meetings and wedding receptions among them We welcomed the Salvation Army for Quiet Days, finishing with a sing-song together, with their band.

So – since our beginnings, the Community has had to adapt from time to time to many changes through the years. Two World Wars have also left their mark. The habit we wear has been brought up-to-date, with slightly shorter skirts, and less complicated caps and wimples. The drip-dry material now used does not need starching and ironing, as in the old days!

Divine Office is now fourfold, instead of our former sevenfold Office, Our main work now is a Life of Prayer, centred round our Daily Eucharist and Offices and Interecessions; helping one another, and our neighbours, with whatever problems are presented to us.

To celebrate our Centenary, on 20 February, 1982, an Ecumenical Eucharist for Friends and other Religious Communities was held in the Chapel at Lindfield. Five Priests concelebrated Mass, the Chief Celebrant being the Bishop of Lewes, himself a monk. Ten Religious Communities were represented: Orders of both men and women; some Anglican and some Roman Catholic. After the Service, there was a buffet lunch, followed later by Vespers and tea. Altogether, it was a very happy day for us.

One of the most notable changes during the past hundred years has been that in the Ecumenical climate. Fifty years ago, a Service such as we had that day, would have been unthinkable. Thanks be to God, indeed!

The façade of Holy Rood Convent, Findon

Surprised by Joy

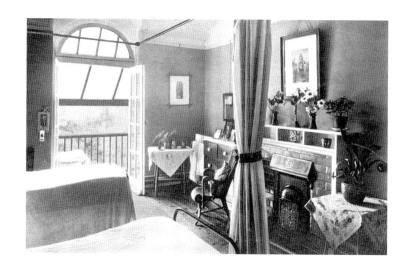

A Guest Room at Findon

A Private Patients' Sitting-room, Findon

A ward at Findon

Aerial view of Findon Convent

Surprised by Joy

Some of our older Sisters, including Sr Winifred, Sr Dorothea, Sr Lena, Sr Hannah, Sr Ethel, Sr Mildred, Sr Gertrude Anna, Sr Gertrude, Sr Bertha, Sr May, Sr Olive, Sr Louise, Sr Stella, Sr Rosina, and Sr Christine Mary – Findon, 1943

Mother Amy and Mother Ethelwyn, CSMV are in the picture – Findon, 1943

*Postulant Louise, Sr Muriel Agnes, Sr Dorothea
and Novice Margaret at Findon, 1943*

*Statue of St Michael at Holyrood
(moved to Lindfield, 1967)*

Surprised by Joy

The Calvary Walk, Findon

Nepcote Lane,
Findon c.1800

The Buxted children, Findon, 1923

The Buxted children, with Sr Bertha of the Cross

Surprised by Joy

Group of Sisters at Findon

A Reunion of the 'Buxted Girls' – now grown up! At Findon

JOHANNESBURG

*Sr Mildred with the Nurses at Jane Furze Memorial Hospital,
Johannesburg, in the late 1940s*

Holy Rood Chapel at Furze Hospital, Johannesburg

3

Sister Jane's own account of the Community

From her entry at the Convent of the Holy Rood, Findon in 1959

The Convent was tucked below the South Downs. It had an impressive front door with its title in large print above it. On the left was the three-storied building of the Nursing Home with its ten-bedded wards and one eight-bedded ward: home for some eighty terminally ill women.

The second and third floors were reached either by a stone staircase, or a lift. On the ground floor were St Mary's Ward and Saint Gabriel's Ward, with bathrooms, toilets and kitchenettes. At the far end of St Gabriel's Ward, divided by a screen, was a large hall. There, many social activities went on, especially at Christmas. We got all the patients in, walking them in wheelchairs or even beds to watch and enjoy an impromptu concert given, and receive gifts from the enormous, imposing Christmas tree Many of the gifts were hand-made by the Sisters throughout the year, often at Recreation Times – homely gifts, such as flannels, hot water bottle covers, handkerchiefs with initials embroidered on them, soap and powder, but they were much appreciated by the patients.

We had wonderful sales of work there, too: a splendid source of income to pay for the upkeep of the Home. These were joyful occasions for meeting friends and Associates, and people from the village.

On the front side of the Home, there was a sun parlour: a covered balcony where the patients could sit and enjoy fresh air and sunshine. There were also balconies on each floor at the front of the building.

The middle floor was for the private patients, with a Kitchen and Sitting Room-cum-Dining Room at the centre of the two passages.

Each ward had access to the Chapel.

The top floor housed Saint Raphael Ward and Saint Michael Ward, and a small passage with one or two rooms leading off it. Here, too, were a large Sitting Room and a little Mortuary, where each coffin was placed, with candles, flowers and a crucifix, until the funeral.

At the end of the passage was the entrance to the Chapel gallery, which housed the organ. The former wind-blown organ had been replaced, by the time I arrived, with an electric organ. Many stories were told about the manual handling of the wind-blown organ, and the Sisters who had to pump it for the organist!

There was also an entrance into the Convent area, where the Sisters slept. That would have been the top corridor with the Sisters' Cells. On the second floor was the Workroom, too. The doors were always closed to any but the Workroom Sisters and those who had business there. It was a bit of a 'holy of holies' place to me, in those early days of my Vocation.

At that time, the Novices were kept much apart from the Sisters and although we worked with them on the wards, we never shared much conversation, apart from what work required. Although we did share many a laugh at some of the situations we found ourselves in!

We had our own Novitiate Common Room, and only joined the Sisters for Sunday Recreation. We sat on low chairs or stools with our knitting and sewing, dumbstruck and awe-struck. We would be listening – as was the custom in our Community at Recreation – to a book, read to us by the Mother or Senior Sister. Or perhaps it would be some item from a newspaper or magazine.

We were never allowed to go to our Cells during the day. We could go into the Chapel or garden. I found this restriction very hard myself. We rose at the Call Bell (which was at 5.30am at Findon, and 6am at Lindfield) and went to Prayer Time in Chapel before the Office of Prime. This was followed by either Mass, or breakfast for those detailed for early ward duty. On the wards, we started with Morning Prayer for the patients. Then we prepared them for breakfast, and went to the kitchenettes, where trays had been laid out ready, with food brought from the main kitchen, if my memory serves me rightly. The patients had breakfast on tables over their beds.

When all this was done and everyone was getting on with their breakfast, we went to Chapel for Terce, leaving our helpers to watch over things and clear away.

After the Office, we went to our separate Common Rooms, for Conference and Instruction for the day. Then we returned to work on the wards, or in the Laundry, or Kitchen, or wherever we were needed, until the midday Office of Sext, before dinner. Every morning, we bathed or washed the patients, got them all dressed and into their chairs, and placed somewhere safe while we made their beds and swept and dusted.

On Fridays, we had to pull the beds and lockers out into the centre of the room, and the walls were mopped down and floors, washed.

Surprised by Joy

The spring clean once a year was a mammoth task – an "all hands on deck" affair. But we had fun, too, and sometimes got up to pranks!

Before going to Midday Office and our own dinner, we had to serve the patients with theirs. Each ward had a hot trolley sent up from the kitchen, and was served out on trays by the Senior Sisters, to be carried round to the patients by we others. In early days, they told us, they had to take the trays from the bottom ward all the way up the stairs to the other wards. In my day, each ward had separate service. Life had become easier, it was said!!

After dinner, we went along to our respective Common Rooms for Recreation and chat amongst ourselves. Or we listened to another Sister read from a book or read an article, while we others sat quietly and got on with our knitting or sewing.

The Novices' afternoon consisted of gardening time; or classes for various subjects connected with our Vocation and growth in knowledge. Or we would take 'the Girls' for a walk. Kind volunteers from the village saw to the patients' teas at 3 pm in each ward. This made for a good relationship between the Convent and the village.

We ourselves went to the Refectory for tea, and then to the Chapel for Vespers.

After Vespers, we went back to the wards to prepare the patients for supper, at about 6 to 6.30, I think. Later, we cleared up the ward kitchens, and then prepared to settle the patients down for the night. When that was done, we said evening prayers with them, before shading the lights.

At that point the night staff took over, and we went off to Compline. We then went to our Cells. The Greater Silence was kept until after breakfast next morning, unless there was an emergency to be dealt with. We also kept a Lesser Silence for three hours in the morning, and one hour in the afternoon, except on festival or special days.

It was quite a tough routine but of course we were younger then, and many pleasant happenings offset the rigour: outings and parties; concerts, and such like.

At the time I entered the Community, early in 1959, Mother Alma Britta was the Mother, and Sister Pauline was our Novice Mistress. The Rev'd Percy Berkley was the Resident Chaplain, and the Rev'd Father Slade, SSJE (Society of St John the Evangelist) was our Warden . The Rt Rev'd Bishop Roger Wilson, of Chichester, was our Visitor.

But change was just over the horizon. We could not maintain the standard of nursing required by the Boards of Nursing. With no aspirants coming forth, and many Sisters ageing, we were eventually forced to give up this work, and find some other service for our Lord.

We were told of the need to find new Homes for our patients, and this was happily accomplished, in due course.

As time grew nearer for change, Mother Alma Britta was replaced by Mother Francesca, CSMV. In the Novitiate were Novice Ursula, Novice Joan, and myself. Soon afterwards, Novice Ursula became Sister, which left me as Senior Novice. Novice Joan had become ill, and finally left. Several Aspirants came after this, but none stayed, except for Sister Ruth and Sister Monica. Then Sister Dorothy May came to us, at our new Convent at Lindfield and was Professed. She had come to us from her recent nursing career and had up-to-date knowledge of drugs and medical treatments. She died of cancer, after only a few years as our Infirmarian. I inherited the task of Infirmarian from her. For a while, I studied medicine almost more than my Bible!

I have not yet recorded that when St Margaret's, Lindfield, was our Branch House for a few years, we used a little room to the right of the front door as our Chapel. The Altar and Tabernacle were in front of a bay window so that as you sat on your chair, you looked out on the grounds below and could see ponies grazing quietly in the paddock. It was a most tranquil sight – except on the morning one of them got over the fence and walked about on the lawn among the flowers!!

That dear little Chapel became Mother's Room when we were resident at Lindfield, and a larger room next door became our Chapel for a time. Our own Chapel was built and consecrated about two years later. The builders had cleverly unblocked a passage and the Cloister into the Chapel was added to the opened-up wall, thus joining the Chapel to the House.

We did our own laundry at Lindfield, and the churches around would bring theirs to us, too. In those days, linen was starched and it was a great challenge. What a relief it was when drip-dry garments came into use! It certainly halved our laundry load. Initially, a lot of time was spent making two summer and two winter Habits for each Sister. However, once done, less mending was involved and the material was hard-wearing and long-lasting. Sister Janet Mary was our seamstress at that time and, with the help of others, did a great job.

Above the Laundry, was Bert and Mary Farmer's flat, which had once housed two or three residents of St Margaret's House, before we all moved from Findon.

Mr Farmer was always 'on hand' when we had any trouble in the Convent, and he was our 'driver'. His great joy was to serve at Mass, and he seldom

Our best White Altar Frontal, made by past Sisters, in their spare time

Holyrood Convent, Lindfield

The Chapel at Lindfield

The Altar and Cross in the Chapel, Lindfield

All the Sisters on the steps of the Chapel, when it was finished

*Sister Jessica and her gardening stall in the greenhouse –
somewhat restored*

*Father Hollowood
with his dog, Julie*

*Mr Farmer,
our treasured handyman
and 'jack of all trades',
with Father Hollowood*

*Sister Helena, Gladys, Mr Reg Sayers, our gardener, Mrs Barbara Sayers
and their daughter, Miranda, at a Children's and Workers' Party
in St Richard's Hall, Lindfield*

Sr Helena and Sr Ruth, in the Lindfield kitchen

*St Mary and the
Holy Child Statue,
made by
Mother Maribel, CSMV*

*Sister Margaret,
sharing a painting class*

Mother Dorothea, Mr Farmer, Sr Dorothy May, Sr Janet Mary
and, in front (the then) Sr Angela

The Calvary,
Lindfield

Brother Simon, OSB, with Sisters visiting Alton Abbey

*Mother Dorothea, Sr Theodora and
Sr Olive, at Lindfield*

Sister Monica

The Nativity – Crib figures made by Mother Maribel,
and set in a life-size shed, Christmas, 1979

A Christmas Party in progress in St Richard's Hall

Hanging out the laundry

The antics of the semi-wild cats at Lindfield gave us much pleasure. They were regularly fed by Sr Monica, for which service they kept us free from mice and rabbits!

Mrs Christine Berkley, Miss Freda Poole and Sr Jessica, at Lindfield

Mother Angela and Mother Doris, doing a bit of 'Gardening Time'!

Celebrating the Installation of Mother Doris – l. to r. Father Hollowood, Mother Doris, Sr Dorothy May, Bishop Eric Kemp, Mother Dorothea, Father Allen (Warden), a guest and Sr Theodora. 31 July, 1985, Lindfield

Mother Doris, getting to grips with the Centenary Cake! 1992

The Apple Walk,
Lindfield

MARRIOTT HOUSE

*Beyond the end of the
balcony rooms and paths
are the Chapel of St
Bartholomew and the
Cemetery, both very old.
The Chapel was re-
opened for our use eight
years ago, on our arrival
there, having been closed
when the Theological
College closed down*

*Marriott House
(now one of the Homes of Barchester Health Care Co. Ltd)*

*A Christmas Party at Marriott House in 1999, with Friends – l. to r.
Sr Jessica, Jennifer Hardwick (daughter), Mother Doris, Anthony
Hardwick, Mother Angela, Sr Margaret, and Sr Ruth*

Sr Christina Mary, Mrs Phyllis Peirce, Mother Doris's cousin, and Mother Angela, Marriott House, at Lindfield

Mother Angela and Sr Margaret with a Friend, Marriott House, 2000

The Cherry Tree, outside our Community Room at Lindfield.
We hung food for the birds on its boughs, and we watched young Green
Woodpeckers and Finches, various Tits, and tree-creepers enjoying it

missed doing so. We were very grateful to him, and to Mary. She was great fun to be with, and often took us out in her car for a run in the country, always finding some interesting spot to take us to.

We also shared the joy of their children growing up, and their grandchildren, when they came along.

We were very sorry when we had to part with them. Sadly, Bert died in 2002, but we still keep in touch with Mary.

The Chaplain's Lodge was at the bottom of the drive, on Park Lane. That, too, had once been the Home of several of St Margaret's ladies. Father Lewis Hollowood was the last Chaplain, and he will stay at the Lodge, now called 'Holy Rood Cottage', as long as he is capable of living alone. We still visit him occasionally.

He has a black and tan King Charles spaniel, though, to keep him company. He says she is the congregation when he says Mass in his little Oratory upstairs! The cottage is separated from the Convent, which is now flourishing as an Autistic Society Home.

Going back to 1967, Mother Francesca, CSMV, was with us as our Mother when we moved to our new Holy Rood Mother House in Lindfield. I have already written about our work there (see pages —), but I will now add a little more about those days.

We wore black habits in the winter. Before they were put away for the summer, they had to be scrubbed inside, especially along the seams, where dust collected. We hung them out on the line, praying that it would gently rain over night, which would make them the right dampness for pressing out and airing next morning! Then, thankfully, we packed them neatly away in newspaper tied with string, until the next winter.

Our summer habits were of light grey cotton. They could be washed, but then had to be half-dried, rolled up, put through starch solution, then unrolled again, for ironing. We played a game with them sometimes, when they had dried too much, while starched. We stood them on the ground, and they remained standing in their own stiffness! It was wonderful when we discarded these for drip-dry habits.

Some years went by before we could recover from the trauma of leaving Findon and settling down to a life without our nursing care. Gradually, however, we found a new Spirituality, and learned to cope with the smaller space and nearer proximity of one another.

It had also become clear that Mother Francesca was now a very sick woman. On reporting matters to Mother General at Wantage, she decided that the time had come to vote for our own Mother, from our own Community. We had been urged to consider this for some time, so the decision was not unexpected.

In 1976, Sister Dorothea of the Cross was voted the first Mother of our Community. Sister Doris became her Assistant and Sister Theodora remained our Bursar. As there was no Novitiate, no Novice Mistress was needed. In later years, when we *did* get some testing their Vocation, the Novitiate was run on very different lines, and Mother Doris instructed the Novices herself, with the help of the Chaplain, when necessary.

So now we had our Retreat and Conference Centre, and we accepted short-term guests. And, at the end of St Richard's Hall, we had the Prophets' Chamber. (A Prophets' Chamber is a small room added on to a home for a visitor. The idea originates in an Old Testament story [2 Kings 4: 8-10] about Elishah and the widow.) Here, Priests could stay for retreats and rest: a service that was much appreciated.

In this way, we met a lot of lovely people, and quite a number of Sisters from other Convents came to us to convalesce or rest, too.

Things began to get difficult in the mid-1980s. In 1985, Mother Dorothea had a stroke and retired from office. Our last Professed Sister, Dorothy May, died on 26th March, 1990 – a great blow to us, as she was our Infirmarian. Mother Doris asked Wendy Compton if she would look after their financial affairs. Mrs Compton was appointed Bursar to the Trustees on 10 December, 1994, by Canon Keith Hobbs, our Warden at that time. In 1995, Mother Doris became ill and confused. Sister Angela then became Mother and I became Assistant, until we had to leave the Convent on 21st December, 1996. On 1st July 1996, Wendy Compton also became our Bursar. She has always been our friend, as well as a great help in sorting out our finances. We owe her a great debt of gratitude.

We struggled on for another two years, the Sisters becoming more and more frail, so that we had to call on Social Services to help us and advise. They sent carers to bath two of our Sisters, Sister Helena and Sister Jessica, once a week. They also arranged for Sister Jessica to go to an activity centre in Haywards Heath once a week, to assess her mental condition, and to see if she would perhaps benefit from the visits.

Sister Janet Mary had become increasingly incapacitated by arthritis. When she damaged an arm, trying to cope for herself with a pulley over her bed, we felt we were causing her more pain than necessary, to carry on that way. She went to be cared for by St Peter's Sisters, Woking, who were then taking in Sisters from other Communities. It was reluctantly, and with great sadness, we had to part with her. We visited her as often as we could.

Then Sister Jessica began to need more and more help, and Sister Mary Faith had fallen and broken her arm That same year, it came to our ears that Chichester Theological College had been closed. Subsequently, it was bought by a Mr and Mrs Perry, to convert into a luxury Retirement Home – Marriott House. We applied to the Perry's, who in fact welcomed our remaining Sisters with open arms, and used to say "Our Home has something no others have – a praying presence of religious Sisters". It had the advantage of a Chapel in the grounds. This was redundant, but the Bishop of Chichester allowed it to be opened again for our use, while there.

We began by sending the Sisters two by two for a short stay, to see how it went. However, God appears to have stepped in at this point, and hurried things on. When the second complement, Mother Angela and Mother Doris (by now retired) were sent, Mother met with an accident and landed in hospital. As it was a week before Christmas week, an urgent message came for me, as Assistant, to pack the necessary luggage for the five remaining Sisters, and get them over to join Mother Doris, at Marriott House.

I hired a very large taxi to take them all away, with their luggage. It was a difficult moment for us all, and Sister Jessica could not understand what was happening. It was bewildering for me, too, suddenly finding myself alone in our Convent. But there was much to be done in the House before I myself could leave.

Mrs Joan Adams, our cook, kindly stayed on to look after me, pack up the Kitchen and dispose of all the food. Wendy Compton also helped us to arrange for packets of foodstuff and the Christmas hampers to go to our workers. These had already been prepared earlier in the year.

The semi-wild cats living with us on the premises could not be left to fend for themselves, and we had high jinks trying to get them all into the cages provided by the RSPCA. I heard later that they had all been taken, and let loose in a garden centre near Brighton, and were very happy there!

Joan stayed with me at night, and we chose the two best bedrooms in the House!! I had the double guest room and Joan had the one next door, both upstairs, overlooking the front lawns. There, we felt safe. I had packed up, and was living out of my cases! It surely was a strange time for us all.

I got up before Joan, to say my Office in Chapel before breakfast. I didn't unlock any doors, though, until I heard Mr Farmer around. He and Mary had moved to a flat in the village, but he came daily to keep an eye on things, and do whatever had to be done about the place. He and Father Hollowood, Joan and I had our dinner together. Rex and Lorraine King, our Associate friends and helpers at Lindfield, came in sometimes to help, or just be a congregation in Chapel, when we had Mass. Rex helped in the garden or helped Bert Farmer, and Lorraine sometimes worked in the kitchen. All their support was much appreciated.

I spent my time between Offices and meals clearing out the Sisters' rooms, and packing cases and bags – whatever I felt the Sisters would like to keep with them in their new Home. Other rooms also had to be cleared, and whatever was questionable, I put in piles together, for the Sisters to attend to when, at some stage, they would come over to retrieve their belongings. Here, I must make note of all the hard work that Mrs Wendy Compton and her helpers put in, after Mother had been over to deal with the disposal of everything, and they were free to get on with the next stage. This was the huge undertaking of disposing of articles in St Richard's Hall and the Organ in Chapel, which had to be dismantled before it could be got into the removal van, brought by the people who wanted it.

Clearing all the tables, stalls and articles in the Chapel and other rooms – an immense operation in itself – was followed by the cleaning-up. In fact, it all took the best part of a year, before it could be left to the new owners!

Not to mention the books! A mammoth task in itself. We are very grateful for all the willing help given to us, to accomplish this task. This sad, but necessary, occupation kept us all busy.

I was to go to St Peter's, to keep Sister Janet Mary company, and help the Community there wherever I could, joining them for Offices and Mass and living alongside, with other Sisters being looked after from other Communities. I was taken over there to share Christmas with them, but I had to return on 27 December. Our Sister Helena, whom we had had to leave in a nursing home at Haywards Heath, too ill to be moved, was dying. I felt I must go to be with her, and do the necessary when the time came. She died the next day, and I did the last Services for her. She looked lovely and at peace in her Habit.

The Chaplain and Mr Farmer were wonderful and helped me to make Sister's funeral arrangements. I let all her relations know, but unfortunately none of them could come to the funeral, owing to heavy snow on the roads, and they lived some distance away. Our own Sisters could not make the journey from Chichester, either, but two Sisters from Woking came to support us, and several of our workers and friends came, too. Joan prepared hot soup for anyone who needed it, after the Cremation Service, before they went home.

I sent copies of the Service and a description of the arrangements, to Sister's relations, with small remembrances from her belongings, for them to treasure. They were most grateful and we still exchange greetings at Christmas and Easter. Sister Helena's brother, Shaun, died last year.

On 23 January 1997, there was to be a meeting of the Trustees at the Convent at Lindfield. I decided to remain there until that was over, and Joan stayed to help. Before going to Woking, I thought I would spend the weekend with my brother in Lamberhurst, Kent. Rex kindly took me over.

I arrived back to find the Convent had been broken into, with much damage done to the doors. A door upstairs I was most grieved about, because the second door to the same room further along the corridor was open, so there had been no need to break the other door down. It was the room just re-decorated for Sister Theodora's return. She had had a severe abdominal operation, then had fallen and broken a leg. After recovery from that, we sent her to convalesce at St Peter's. Sister had a fit, and died there. She had been our Bursar for many years and it was a sad loss.

Nothing was taken from upstairs, but the office was a mess. They had broken in, and blown open the safe door. The padding stuff surrounding it was all over the floor, and the money contents of the safe had gone – although fortunately, there was not much money to take.

I was sorry for Mr Farmer and the Chaplain, who discovered the break-in when they came on duty. Anyway, the last two nights, I slept at Joan's home and we both went back together and left together in the evening for those last two days before the Meeting.

All went well at the Meeting. Father Keith Hobbs, our Warden, brought Mother Angela with him, and took her back to Chichester afterwards. Joan and I cleared things up. Then I left for St Peter's, which was to be my new home with Sister Janet Mary and the other Sisters.

So ended another thirty years of our Community life.

★ ★ ★ ★ ★

Our Mother House was now Marriott House. Father Hobbs was nearby to guide them through the difficult time of cultural shock and change. He came over to see us regularly at Woking, and used to say that we were "the outriders of the Community". He was a great help to us all, until his death in 2000.

We continued to support one another in our separate places, by letter or telephone, sharing our news and expectations through sadness, sickness and joys, too.

In July, 2002, the unexpected happened again: and Sister Janet Mary and I found we had to leave St Peter's, as their infirmary was to be closed within the year. It was a great blow also for St Peter's Sisters themselves.

Sister Janet Mary and I packed up to return again, on 22 August, to the bosom of our Community. Mrs Perry had assured us that there were rooms and a welcome for us, and that they could manage Sister Janet Mary's needs.

Although the change was traumatic for us both, Sister was happy to be with the Community again, and loved to talk with so many new people. She was a joyful presence for the three weeks she was with them, and they all appreciated her sense of fun. Thankfully, it was summer and we were able to spend a lot of time in the garden during the days. Sister was happy, doing her craft work among other residents, laughing and chatting away. On 11 September, Sister collapsed with abdominal pain and was taken to hospital. She died peacefully on 15 September.

Sister Janet Mary and I had been together many years, and she taught me many things, and shared the memories of her years in the Australian outback, as a Religious Sister. She was greatly loved by the friends she left behind in Australia, and corresponded with them to the end.

Now there were only three of us left to carry on, all of us over eighty years old, but doing our best to keep up the tradition of the Servants of the Cross. Who knows what the future held for us in these very insecure days?

'The best is yet to be. Alleluia!'

The first indication of more change ahead was when Father Desmond Curson collapsed while leading us through the Stations of the Cross, on Good Friday, 2002. Mother and I and one or two of the congregation had to finish the Stations ourselves, Sister Margaret also being ill at this time. Father Desmond never recovered so that we found our Communion Service could only be held on two weekdays, when our Warden, John Lyon, came to celebrate for us, and on Sundays.

Then, on 23 April, 2003, our dear Sister Margaret died peacefully in hospital. She had not been at all well for some time, but kept going bravely, to the best of her ability. That left only two of us to carry on – Mother Angela and myself. This means that the past few months have been a period of finishing-off, so that we can start again. Without regrets, to complete the course God has set for us at the 'tail-end', as it were, of our Community on this earth.

It was our custom to hold our Associates and Friends Festival Gathering on the nearest Saturday after the 14 September each year: The Exaltation of the Cross. So, on 20 September, 2002, we held our last Gathering, and said a formal farewell to them all. It was a very special day. We had the Rt Rev'd Bishop John Hind, of Chichester, to officiate at the Concelebrated Mass. He also kindly gave the address. Afterwards, we all went for a buffet lunch at Marriott House, and a get-together. We displayed some photographs of the Community for them to look at. It was a very happy occasion for us all. In the afternoon, we met again in Chapel, for Choral Evensong and Benediction: a fitting end to the day.

Two days later, we went to spend a week at St Mary's Gatehouse, Wantage, to go through our archives, housed there, and to finish the research for this short history of our Community, published so that our Associates will have something to remember us by, and maybe bring comfort to others in like circumstances. It has been a most satisfying task.

We prayed about our future, and came to believe that it lay where we were: retired and ageing Sisters, with a small ministry of just 'being a praying presence' among other ageing men and women. We would remain faithful to our vows. The Chapel of St Bartholomew was an oasis for our use. We keep a Book for many people from many places, in England and abroad, who have worshipped in it, or have been baptised here, returned to see it again, and recorded their feelings. The Chapel has been a place of prayer for a long time.

We neither of us really knew what the future held for us, but we know God is faithful, and He is love, and that we can safely place ourselves in His keeping. It seems that he has brought us into a new kind of Community, in which to honour and obey Him in the Cross of the suffering Christ …

However, it could be said that 'retirement' has its perks!

We have television in our rooms. We can go out for a walk or to the shops whenever we like. We can accept invitations from kind friends, to dinner or to go on outings, and join in the various activities laid on for us by the staff here at Marriott House, if we wish. And all in Obedience! So long as we make time for our religious duties and commitments. These, in fact, fill up much of our day as we are getting slower now, which is what we all get, when we grow old. The discipline comes in when we have to leave a programme on TV we like, to go to Chapel, or to an activity arranged for us all to share in the House!

LINDFIELD

Our Cells being prepared at St Margaret's House, Lindfield, ready for our arrival

Our Cells ready for occupation.
The cross marks where the Chapel would be added, in due course

Surprised by Joy

Old greenhouse (once a vine house), Lindfield, in the garden as it was

'Mother's Room' – the first, temporary, Chapel at Lindfield

Laying the Foundation Stone of our Chapel at Lindfield

Ducks at the bottom of the garden, when we first moved to Lindfield in 1967, with the House in the background

Surprised by Joy

St Richard's Hall

Leisure Time at Lindfield

The up-to-date Laundry! (in the 1970s)

*Father and
Mrs Berkley*

Surprised by Joy

Father Sargent, Bishop Bell, Father Stothart and Father Berkley

The Sewing Room, Lindfield

*Simple printing done at
Home, Lindfield*

*The Community of the Servants of the Cross, Lindfield, c. 1998
back row, l. to r. Sr Theodora, Sr Jane, Sr Dorothy May, Sister Janet Mary,
Sr Angela, and Sr Helena
Front row, l. to r. Sr Christina Mary, Mother Doris, Sr Monica, Sr Margaret,
Sr Mary Faith, and Sr Ruth*

Surprised by Joy

4

Sister Margaret's memories
(written in 2003)

My earliest recollection of Holy Rood Convent was in 1923 when, as a little girl of eight, my mother sought help for her large family at St Mary's Home, Buxted. It was a Branch House of the St Mary the Virgin Wantage Community, helped by some of the Holy Rood Sisters. There was Sister Christina Mary, then a Novice in the Community, Sister Bertha and Sister Priscilla. We were sometimes taken to Holy Rood, to put on an entertainment for the patients. I received Confirmation and First Communion there in June, 1924: joyful days, never to be forgotten.

In due time, I came to test for my Vocation at Findon, in 1940. The war was going on, and we had to take turns of duty up on the flat roof of the Convent, and had to plot the course of planes passing over. I recall seeing one enemy plane chased by one of our planes, and brought down at Bost Hill.

Eventually, in November, 1940, I was clothed as a Novice. Sister Rhoda was the Senior Novice then, Sister Patricia, CSMV, was Novice Mistress, and Mother Ethelwyn, CSMV, was the Mother. In 1944, I was Professed by the Rt Revd George Bell, the then Bishop of Chichester.

I kept up with the 'Buxted girls' for many years, but some have gone to 'higher service' now. And now I myself, at eighty-eight, have to 'serve' by being 'served'. Not easy for me!

5

Mother Angela's memories
(written in 2002)

I arrived at the front door of Findon Convent on 24th January, 1947, feeling very nervous. I was met by Sister Pauline, whom I knew slightly, and so I soon felt more at home.

It was a very cold, white world and, in those days, I really felt the cold. (Today, at eighty-one, I do not feel the cold much. Indeed, I'm often boiling hot, when others are freezing!)

The night of my arrival at Findon, I was asked if I had brought a hot water bottle with me. "No," I replied, "I did not think it would be allowed." So they found me one, and packed me off to bed, after Compline.

Next morning, I rose with the Call Bell. I had been told to go to the Chapel for Prime and Mass, then to breakfast – for which, by that time, I was ready! I soon got used to the regular routine of the day. We were sometimes sent out for walks, taking with us the 'Alton girls' – the girls we cared for. They were very good, but could get up to pranks, so we had to keep a watchful eye on them!

Somehow, I was always being caught by Mother Amy running up the stairs two at a time, and made to come back and walk up like a lady.

We enjoyed our Novitiate days very much. Our Novice Mistress was always thinking up things for us to do, for a change: picking primroses at Easter-time, to make a little Easter garden; taking us for picnics on our Anniversaries; gardening, and taking us autumn plum- and apple-picking. These were all 'outlets', and good for us.

The routine seemed hard work at times, but always fun, as we were young and full of the joys of spring.

We were given a book to enter the 'times' of what we did at every moment of the day. Actually, it was a great help, for it meant we could never be idle. The days were long, but good and rewarding.

I remember when we had to leave Findon for Lindfield. St Margaret's House was not quite ready for us all, so Sister Mary Grace, Sister Jessica, Sister Janet Mary and I had to go to Wantage. We certainly didn't want to go, but we knew we had to. So off we went. Once we had found our way about, we all settled down there for three months, helping on the East Wing of the Convent, which was the nursing wing for sick Sisters; or in the Laundry, or wherever we were needed. But how wonderful it was when Mr Farmer came to take us Home!

I recall some very pleasant times at Lindfield, such as the time when Mr Farmer took Mother Dorothea, Sister Doris, Sister Jessica, Sister Margaret and myself to Mr Wood's farm to 'pick-up' the potatoes to keep us going for the winter. We took flasks of drinks and packed lunches with us.

Some days, in summer, we also went to 'pick-up' strawberries. We picked pounds to take home. Then there was the time when Sister Pauline and I painted the walls (and ourselves!) with green paint. And I must not forget how Mother Dorothea, Sister Margaret, Sister Ethel and Sister Jane all joined in the twenty-mile Chichester walk, towards the upkeep of the Cathedral for one year. It was tough going towards the end, but we finally made it!

We must not omit to mention the outings we arranged for our patients, and the concerts and country dancing for their pleasure, both at Findon and at Lindfield. We enjoyed the parties in St Richard's Hall at Christmas, and the piano recitals. All the hard work involved was very worthwhile, when we saw joy on the faces around us.

2002

Here at Marriott House, we do not do these things – they are done for us. We share the fun, the ups and downs, the frustration and pain of our imperfect society. In such a life, we feel very close to Our Lord; helping each other to be faithful to the end.

> *'A whole I planned.*
> *Youth shows but half.*
> **Trust God; see All;**
> *Be not afraid.'*
>
> **Robert Browning**

6

Friends and Helpers

Before we end this unfinished story of our Community, we must put on record the debt of gratitude we owe to our faithful Associate Members, from its beginnings to the present day. At times, we were deeply aware of the sustaining support of their prayer, as well as of their practical help in various ways, and of their friendship and love, in Christ.

Thanks be to God for the Associates and Friends whom He called to support us through our Pilgrimage!

One other group deserves our grateful remembrance: members of the Salvation Army at Burgess Hill who were regular visitors to our Lindfield Convent. They brought their band and songsters to entertain us, and share the Gospel Message. They also told us various stories of their work among people, which interested us greatly. Sometimes, we welcomed them into our Chapel to spend a Quiet Day, just in their own way. Afterwards, we were invited to join them in St Richard's Hall, for a time of fellowship and singing.

> **'Our Lord has said,**
> **"Gather up the fragments that remain,**
> **that nothing be lost".'**

Our lives are made up of so many fragments, but Jesus will gather them all up and save them for Eternal Life. We will be SURPRISED BY JOY!

7

Poem composed for us by a Swedish monk staying in the House, about 1944

All our longings and tears,
All our shadows and fears.
So much that will be left undone.
Many new roads yet to come.

All these efforts and all these years,
All our blessings and all our cheers.
So much that will be gently done.
O great kindly Light
lead
us
on.

Brother Benedict

8

For those who remember some of our Community members

We remember our dear departed Mothers and Sisters with great affection. We recall their foibles and graces, and many of the stories attached to them, as their families do. We are all individuals and unique in God's sight, and some little oddity or saying recalls them vividly to mind. I can of course only speak for those I lived with.

Sister Ethel – We will ever remember her obstinate refusal to say the fifth verse of Psalm 51: 'Surely in wickedness I was brought to birth; and in sin, my mother conceived me'! And we have a little book of Homilies she wrote for a church magazine – I think it was the *Christian Herald*.

Sister Christina Mary – We remember her Scottish dourness, but her delight at being photographed at parties, and her devotion to the Blessed Sacrament.

Sister Olive – for her lovely, coloured script cards for the Community's Anniversary, and individual Profession Day cards; also, her stories of belonging to the Chipperfield's circus family, standing on the back of a circus horse in the ring as a small child, and other wondrous tales.

Mother Dorothea – for her Motherliness, and sense of fun. Although she was very strict about the Rule of Silence, and urged us to do better!

Sister Stella – for her fastidiousness, and endearing ways.

Sister Hannah – Well, she was just Sister Hannah! Very knowledgeable she was, and she loved talking of her family.

Sister May – She was a wonderful, trained seamstress. She had been a teacher, I believe, and she used to teach 'the Girls' to dance and act in plays.

Sister Mary Grace – A motherly person, and very reassuring to be nursed by. Strict but fair. She used to say: "Well, you may ask, but you may not get! If you don't ask, you won't get"!

Sister Bertha – A quiet, dignified person. A willing listener, and kindly.

Sister Mildred – A gay little person, and a wonderful cook. I recollect being in the kitchen with her for a short spell, at Findon, and seeing the huge vats of butter for making pancakes or toad-in-the-hole; and large tins for making milk puddings for everyone. She showed me how to judge the amount of rice grains to place in each tin – a great art.

Sister Lena – I remember I had just arrived at Holy Rood, and Sister asked me to go to her in her Cell, where she had been ill for some time. I greeted her, and her remark was "Well, she knows how to give the kiss of peace, anyway"!!

Sister's funeral was the first I was allowed to share in the walk behind the bier, on foot, to the Community burial ground in Findon Cemetery. The Sisters had gone up in the evening before the funeral, to put flowers all round the inside of the grave, a custom I had never met before.

Sister Rhoda – When I came into the Community, Sister was walking on sticks. She had had a fall and broken her leg, and she was also full of arthritis. She had been Organist and Choir Mistress for the Community. I remember her story of how once she was travelling by train to see her sister, and her veil got caught in the door and was torn off her head. She laughed uproariously when she told this story.

Sister Freda – I know little about her, apart from the fact that she had a little room which housed the Girls' things, at the end of the kitchen corridor. I think I remember a story of her chasing a mouse in the storeroom. She was loved by everyone.

Sister Theodora – a mainspring of the Community. She looked after our finances, and also nursed us. She was well-known for her cold 'recipes'!! They were very potent, and meant to be an instant cure! Her sudden, unexpected death left us without a Bursar, until Mrs Wendy Compton took over that job.

Sister Jessica – Well, she was "a caution", as they say! Very loveable but a bit of a handful at times. She had a great attachment to Paddington Bear in her latter years (from the book, and from the TV programme before the 6pm news, at that time). She was remembered for her lovely, warm smile for everyone, and won the hearts of all who came in contact with her.

Mother Doris – a loving and caring Mother of the Community. She kept us laughing over some little tale she remembered, and leaves a happy memory behind her of a good religious example. She had a wonderful repartee, too. People at Marriott House have often spoken to me of her peaceful, calm expression.

Sister Pauline – was Irish, charming and winsome. As a Novice Mistress, she was thorough and a little strict, but had a warm heart if anyone was in trouble or distress.

Sister Margaret – had had many setbacks in recent years, but she went on courageously in her witness to Christ among us. She 'slowed up' considerably, but was ready for anything that came her way. It was a joke among us that she got "held up by her tongue"! She invariably arrived late, and puffed out! Up to only a year ago, she was able to travel around by public transport, and was our representative at various religious gatherings and conferences. She often went to Chichester Cathedral and was known to nearly everyone serving there.

Sister Lucy – I heard she had been a hard worker, if obstinate, attempting tasks beyond her strength. Once, the Chaplain had 'forty fits', walking along the drive, as he saw Sister leaning out of a third-floor window to clean the outside. It is good to know she is now where no pain or trouble besets her any more.

Sister Mary Faith – What a wonderful talent she had in her tiny hands, working with clay and other materials; making Statues and artificial flowers, beads and coloured ribbons until she was 80 years old. She then declared herself "retired and doing no more work". And she didn't! However, for all her stubborn ways, she was much loved, and we grieved at her loss of mind and purpose in her later days. Her heart was surely in the right place, in God's care.

Sister Janet Mary – She came to us after many years' service in a Community working in the Australian outback. She had many gifts to give to the Community and served it well, despite being a cripple. What is it we most remember of her? Perhaps her availability, especially as her condition worsened in latter years. She was a comfort to many people, with her matter-of-fact attitude to life, and her encouragement, and the delightful twinkle in her eyes.

Sister Helena – a gentle little soul, always eager to help others. As we were coming to the end of our life at Lindfield, Sister became increasingly sick. To give her something to do, she was put in charge of the workroom. Gradually, we began to realise our mending never came back to us…Sister had given it to her favourite Sister of the moment! She was very sweet and loved a joke, even against herself. We miss her, and the moments of pleasure she gave us, and the laughter.

Sister Ruth – She was very clever, and was wonderful with crosswords and at scrabble. She was a great cook, too, and I enjoyed many years working with her in the kitchen at Lindfield. Sister was punctilious about her religious duties. Hers was a very exact and upright personality.

But she was also very loving and compassionate, and a good companion, with many interesting things to say of life, as I remember.

Sister Monica – She came late in life to the Community, having had to care for elderly parents. She came from my own town of Oswestry, in Shropshire, so I felt a bond with her, but she was very much her own person. She lived for her music and playing the organ for us, and at All Saints' Church, Highbrook, nearby. She loved animals, creatures of all kinds. At Lindfield, it was Sister's job to feed the cats we had at Lindfield. We would see her out in all weathers in an old mack and wellingtons, leading the cats, their tails in the air, winding round her feet, to the place where she had elected to feed them. It was an amusing sight.

Sister Dorothy May – came to us straight from her nursing, I think, under the guidance of our then Warden, Father Derek Allen. She was an excellent Infirmarian.

I remember her once saying "I hope I shall be alive when the New Century comes. It will be very exciting!" She was greatly interested in progress, and the things of nature. As a Novice in those days, she was not apart from the Sisters because it was not practical then. She served us all well, and we are sorry she did *not* see the New Century.

Last, but not least:

Mother Angela – A gentle and sweet person, she meets all her troubles and worries with firm trust in God's goodness and protection. She has a motherly concern for me, as we live our last days together. Many a time, she will say to me: "Do not give up. Just trust in God." And I find I can do just that.

> Grow old along with me!
> The best is yet to be,
> the last of life, for which the first was made.
> Our times are in His hand
> Who saith "A whole, I planned.
> Youth shows but half; Trust God;
> see all, nor be afraid.

from *Rabbi Ben Ezra* by **Robert Browning**

9

Remembered and known – Mothers and Superiors, Wardens, Visitors, and Chaplains

We would like to put on record our gratitude for the guidance through the years of the MOTHERS AND SUPERIORS lent to us by the Community of St Mary the Virgin, Wantage, by their Mother Generals. Many we ourselves do not know personally, but we would like to name those we do:

Mother Annie Louisa   1932

Mother Maribel   1940

Mother Marion Frances   1952

Mother Alma Brita   1954

Mother Francesca   1963

with their Superiors, who also helped us until our own Mother Dorothea of the Cross was elected from own Sisters, on the advice of Mother Barbara Charis, the then Mother General at Wantage.

OUR PAST AND PRESENT WARDENS

Those we recall by sight:

The Rev'd Miles Sargent 1940s

Father Slade, SSJE 1950s

Father Manson, SSJE 1968, followed by

Father Cyril Wooley, SSJE

The Rev'd Derek Allen

Canon Keith Hobbs and, finally,

The Rev'd John Lyon 2004

OUR VISITORS – especially those whom we ourselves recall:

The Rt Rev'd George Bell

The Rt Rev'd Roger Wilson

The Rt Rev'd Eric Kemp, and

The Rt Rev'd John Hind,

all of Chichester Diocese.

The Rt Rev'd John Hind is the present, and probably the last, Visitor to our Community.

FORMER CHAPLAINS – whom we can recall personally:

The Rev'd Percy Berkley

The Rev'd Ernest Starkey

The Rev'd Mark Shirley

The Rev'd Lewis Hollowood

The Rev'd Stephen Guise, and

The Rev'd John Lyon, our last Warden in 2004, when we move to St Katherine's House, Wantage.

N.B.   The dates may not all be exact, but they are fairly accurate. When I entered the Community in 1959, Mother Jane Margaret, CSMV, was Mother General and, after her retirement through ill health, Mother Barbara Charis, CSMV, was Mother General.

The present Mother General is
Mother Barbara Charis, Junior, CSMV

10

Founder of our Home in Fulham

Dean Butler (Wantage) and Mother Lucy, CSMV, at Fulham, in 1877,

as recorded in 'Butler of Wantage' by the Sisters of Wantage (ref. page 92)

11

Our Own Mothers of the Servants of the Cross

Mother Dorothea	4th May, 1968
Mother Doris	1985
Mother Angela	1995 –

12

Letter to Associates and Friends for their Final Festival

20 September, 2003

This year will be the last of our gatherings together in Chichester. What can we say, Mother and I, to mark this stage of our journey – and yours, so closely associated with us in love and dedication to showing forth the Glory of the Cross of Christ, our Lord and Master, to all with whom we live and come in contact?

As I think on this, I call to mind the shock we had on going to Chapel one morning recently, to find the Himalayan Holly Tree – one of a pair in the garden which have been there for more than 100 years, seemingly to guard that lovely space – was no more. It was thought children had been playing in its branches and weakened it, so that it had broken in half at the root a week before, and was now laying its great bough across the pathway, with its head across the Chapel wall. Its foliage was like a great hedge along the path, almost to the gate, full of tiny blossom, the sun tipping the top with gold.

Surprised by Joy

A week later, there was an empty space, and just a tiny tree stump.

Yet, from the middle of the stump, a twig of green leaves and blossom rose up triumphant. Surely a hope of life to come, for that stricken tree.

So it is for our Community of the Servants of the Cross – likewise, struck down in the world's estimation – but still, surely, a 'branch' thriving onward in that unseen world to come; kept for us in the heavens in Jesus Christ, our Saviour and Redeemer of the World.

It had been our desire to have a small booklet on the history of our Community for you all to buy as a keepsake. But it was suggested that with a little more delving into our Archives, 'it could be a worthy contribution to the records of Communities' such as ours.

'Moreover, the many people who are depressed, and rightly so, by the appalling tragedies of world and national events over the past three years, could find peace, pleasure and encouragement in their lives from not only the pure simplicity, but also the fun, in these writings.'

Therefore we decided to do this, and hopefully, the History will be on sale in the not-too-distant future. We will keep you informed.

Meanwhile, may these words spur you on. And may they be a means to express our thanks for the loving and generous support you have given to us in the 120-plus years of our growth and witness on earth, to the glory of God's work in his Son.

God bless and keep you all in the years ahead.

Crux – in – Corde

+

Core – in – Cruce

from Mother Angela of the Cross,

Sister Jane of the Cross,

and all departed Brethren of the Servants of the Cross (1882-2003)

Footnote

Since writing about our possible future, an important decision has been taken. On 21 October, 2003, we had a meeting to discuss how we should go forward, now that we are down to just Mother Angela and myself. We have accepted the invitation of Mother Barbara Charis, CSMV to end our days with them in their retirement nursing home at St Katherine's, Wantage.

We have left all the arrangements to Father John, our Acting Warden/Chaplain. The move will probably not be until March of April, 2004, but we are preparing ourselves for any likely, earlier date. One never knows. We went for a few days to St Katherine's in late January, 2004, to see where we will be, and to have our medical needs assessed.

It is a lovely situation, and we will have daily Mass and share the fivefold Office in Chapel. Our spiritual needs will be met, and Father John will visit us regularly. There is room for visitors to stay if need be, and we will be near the Wantage shopping centre, library, and Parish Church.

It will be sad to leave our friends in Chichester, including our fellow residents in Marriott House, but there will be means of keeping in touch, I'm sure. We have to 'move on' when God has another purpose for us, but we remain One in Him always.

> *'While we have youth in our hearts … we can never grow old. Those who express joy and zest for living and life, in our sad world, are not only wonderfully inspiring people to be around, but they also remind us that it is how we feel on the inside that really matters. Not what happens on the outside.'*

Surprised by Joy